Chic Country Style

Chic Country Style

Denise McGann

Sterling Publishing Co., Inc. New York
A Sterling/Chapelle Book

Chapelle, Ltd.:

• Owner: Jo Packham

• Editor: Ray Cornia

• Art Director: Karla Haberstich

• Editorial Director: Caroll Shreeve

• Staff: Areta Bingham, Kass Burchett, Marilyn Goff, Holly Hollingsworth, Susan Jorgensen, Emily Kirk, Barbara Milburn, Karmen Quinney, Cindy Stoeckl, Kim Taylor, Sara Toliver, and Desirée Wybrow

If you have any questions or comments, please contact:
Chapelle, Ltd., Inc., P.O. Box 9252, Ogden, UT 84409
   (801) 621-2777 • (801) 621-2788 Fax
   e-mail: chapelle@chapelleltd.com
   web site: www.chapelleltd.com

This volume is meant to stimulate decorating ideas. If readers are unfamiliar or not proficient in a skill necessary to attempt a project, we urge they refer to an instructional book specifically addressing the required technique.

Photo on half title page by Jesse Walker

Library of Congress Cataloging-in-Publication Data

McGann, Denise.
   Chic country style / Denise McGann.
      p. cm.
   Includes index.
   ISBN 0-8069-8937-8
   1. Decoration and ornament, Rustic. 2. Interior decoration. I. Title

NK2195.R87 .M38 2002
747--dc21

                                                      2002030684

10 9 8 7 6 5 4 3 2 1

Published by Sterling Publishing Co., Inc.
387 Park Avenue South, New York, NY 10016
©2003 by Denise McGann
Distributed in Canada by Sterling Publishing
c/o Canadian Manda Group, One Atlantic Avenue, Suite 105
Toronto, Ontario, Canada M6K 3E7
Distributed in Great Britain by Chrysalis Books
64 Brewery Road, London N7 9NT, England
Distributed in Australia by Capricorn Link (Australia) Pty. Ltd.
P.O. Box 704, Windsor, NSW 2756, Australia
Printed and Bound in China
All Rights Reserved

Sterling ISBN 0-8069-8937-8

Contents

Introduction

Country style has evolved over the years to where it is no longer just about duck and cow motifs, although in some types of country those still exist. It has come to mean a comfortable, personalized, eclectic type of style. There are no hard-and-fast rules to this kind of decorating, and it is not limited to any particular area of the country.

Whether you live in the suburbs, the city, or actually in the country, you can decorate country-style. This book features different examples of rooms and focal points. It is meant to inspire you to develop your own chic country style, starting with ideas found here.

Country—is it a place you can find on a map? Is it a style that is so defined that each time you see it you know exactly what it is? Is it a nostalgic recall of a special place and time with a loved one? Or is it a state of mind, a place in the spirit, a home for your very soul?

Country today has become more synonymous with a feeling of comfort than associated with a particular decorating style. Country is no longer simply owning a weathered wood cabin on the edge of a mountain river that is decorated in Rustic Chic. Country is more than visiting a small cozy bungalow on a secluded beach that is styled all in the simplest of whites, or dreaming of a thatched-roof cottage whose interior is as beautiful as the English-style gardens that surround it. Country has become a place where peaceful hours are spent relaxing on an old-fashioned front porch, where books are read on comfortable chintz sofas, and where meals are enjoyed around large wooden tables when family and friends are present. It is a place where a quieter rhythm is enjoyed and the focus is on the more natural elements of nature. It is the use of simple materials that create a natural elegance, combined with utilitarian objects and timeless treasured antiques. It is built around a theme of family, home, and friends. It is any style you choose to focus on or create from a combination; but one whose tone and quality must be uncomplicated, imaginative, without geographical boundaries, nostalgic, utilitarian, and most of all inviting and completely livable.

Blue & White Country

Color It Country

The color of country—is it always the same? Is it one specific shade or predetermined palette of colors that are the backdrop for a particular decorating style? Or is it any single tone or combination of colors for which the only criteria is that they evoke the essence of a casual yet elegant ambience with a style that is, by any definition, comfortable.

Blue and white are one of those combinations of colors which typify true country style without boundaries or limitations. It is universally loved whether it be in a cottage by the ocean or a cabin in the mountains. It may be the way something is painted in a home where the theme is strictly country casual or one in which the guests are surrounded by the elegant porcelains of the Orient. Blue and white are the colors of nature—the sky that mystifies us and the waters that replenish our daily lives. These two colors are ageless—the early Chinese emperors wore blue as they worshiped the skies—in addition to their being associated with the colors of eternity, infinity, and virtue. They are mystical and romantic, yet always pragmatic. Blue and white are perfect for any style of comfortable country decorating.

Comfortable country to some equals a large chair in which to read, an unlimited supply of books from which to choose, and a sense of casualness so that one can be truly relaxed. Books are not only an escape that can be enjoyed time and again, but they are a popular accent in country decorating. Whether they are arranged neatly on perfectly painted shelves, stacked in seeming disorder on floors and tabletops, or covered with paper, leather, lace, or velvet so as not to be read but visually enjoyed, books can be central to styling any country room.

The books, at left, were ones whose titles were not that important and whose authors are unknown, but the home owner's passion for reading prevented her from parting with them. So that they could be used as an accent in a room filled with books, their covers were sheathed with colored sheets of paper chosen to match the decor. Use temporary archival tape that can be easily removed and will not yellow with age to avoid leaving discoloration marks on the book's inside end papers.

When stacking books on a shelf, use them as a focal point for a particular decorating scheme. Here, these books are used as a backdrop for the two white pitchers and their serving tray. This tray was made by decoupaging a sheet of wrapping paper to a simple unfinished pine tray. The tray was then "washed" with diluted blue acrylic paint, wiped to the desired level of color, sealed with acrylic, then handles were added.

While this arrangement is both clean and practical, some prefer to soften such powerful focal points with flowers or thick and colorful fabric accessories such as place mats, stuffed dolls, handmade quilts, or exquisitely crocheted coasters or doilies.

Whether the dining room is formal or informal, large or small, sharing the family meal should be enjoyed in comfortable surroundings. Because country style can be an endless choice of possibilities of how to obtain the same comfort, two choices for small dining tables are shown here. The table setting to the left is created in all white with rustic French-style earthenware and simple white table and chairs, while the small dining table to the right is more of an eclectic display of vintage white and blue china with the guests being seated in more-formal chairs. Both would be fashionable country choices for the very same room.

When decorating your own country-style dining room, do not be restricted by traditional dining-room styles. Here in this oversized room that is not only used for dining but for food preparation and entertaining, a large Neoclassic console is positioned in the center of the room with two smaller tables on either side.

It is never more true that "the kitchen is the heart of the home" than in country-style decorating. The colors that are chosen and the style that is selected must both be ones that fit a family's constantly changing life-styles, no matter what their ages and needs may be.

White and blue are surely one of the most popular combinations of all kitchen colors. They are cool colors in the face of the kitchen heat; they are clean colors in an area where food is being prepared and served, and they are the beautiful natural colors of nature's sky and necessary water sources where our food is grown and harvested.

The kitchen itself can be predominately wood in architectural and furniture components, like the one on the facing page, or it can be tiled like the examples shown here. It doesn't matter which is selected because both are natural, versatile, easy to clean, and timeless. Tile tables are easy to create with a number of mosaic instruction books that are available, and tiling a wall around a small built-in hutch is a technique that has been popular in Europe for centuries.

When decorating your country kitchen or dining room, plan for a little surprise by using everyday items in unexpected ways as a main design element. For example above, woven picnic baskets and a fringed throw are arranged with a bouquet and a potted plant to form a dining centerpiece between meals. An old hutch serves as a utilitarian place to store kitchen linens and a substantial decorative accent for a room with strong architectural elements.

Accent pieces in the kitchen can also be somewhat of a surprise. Put your dish soap in a tall blue bottle with glass grapes, as above, strung on a ring draped around the bottle's neck. Kitchen hand soap can be handmade and kept handy in an urn birdfeeder or delicately wrapped in tissue and placed in a small nest with feathers and an egg glued on top. Coasters can be used not only for glasses but for many kitchen items. Those at right were made by using photocopied wine labels and transferring them onto tumbled marble tiles.

Whether you are a great cook, the perfect hostess, or someone who usually "orders in," whatever is served tastes so much better when the room in which it is served is casually "decorated" with the aprons that are the signature of a professional cook. They are a very "arty touch" that makes every meal every day just a little bit more "gourmet."

22

Any home with brick walls can be made to appear as if it were part of a quaint French country inn by simply whitewashing the bricks. It is an old technique that allowed for easy upkeep and always made the kitchen appear to be clean and freshly painted. Fanciful vintage towels, antique bottles and baskets, old hats that were once used to shade country ladies while they gathered fruits from their gardens are pieces that add a touch of authenticity and a hint of another time and place.

Don't forget to place your fruit in a basket that has small labels—it will look as if you just picked it up at the farmer's market—and "plant" your garden flowers inside in your favorite mixing bowl. The antique milk bottles can actually be used to serve milk with the breakfast cereal, and the vintage towels that hang in the window can be used as place mats and napkins.

23

In a country home details are important. Storage boxes, for example, must be as beautiful as if they still contained fancy vintage hats. A stack of matching toile hat boxes can be used to store anything from unused dishes to mismatched silverware. Select a paper that coordinates with the room.

To cover your own hat boxes, select a favorite wall- or gift paper. Gather decoupage glue, scissors, and glue brushes. Measure the height of the box and add 1". Measure around the circumference of the box and add ¾". Cut paper to these measurements. Measure the top of the lid and add 1". Cut. Measure height and circumference of lid lip and add ¾". Cut paper to these measurements. Roll glue onto paper for box side. Lay box side onto paper with ½" of the paper extending from top and bottom of box. Smooth paper around box allowing the paper to overlap at the ends. Fold excess paper over the top of the rim and the bottom of the box. Repeat process for lid. Arrange the boxes on a shelf or stacked on the floor. Any place that you want to create a focal point with the boxes can be made more intentional with the addition of harmonious items, such as the blue and white vase above.

The back door of your home often leads to the kitchen—which is usually the most popular room in the house. Which is why it is so important to make certain that this entrance is one of beauty and practicality. Have umbrellas for guests who are leaving in a rainstorm, a coatrack that is not only for coats but to hang favorite vintage pieces, and small pieces of art that can be enjoyed while coats are being buttoned and good-bye hugs and kisses are shared. Keep this area clean, organized, and always welcoming. It can be both the first impression as well as the last impression a visitor or family member may have of you, your home, and your family. As they enter or leave, they should have feelings of comfort, security, and safety, both while inside and to take with them into their day.

Patriotic Country

My Country

Patriotic country is a style that entails a faith in God and country, a sense of individualism, the tenacity of perseverance, a wealth of resourcefulness, the foundation of basic values, an abundance of good sense, an honest sense of humor, and the comforts of everyday life. It is a style that need not be only American in origin; it can be French, or English, or South African. It is simply a use of that which is of a patriotic nature; so if you live in a country other than the USA, substitute your flags for these and place your country's historical artifacts where they can be enjoyed and their stories of history can be remembered daily.

Good down-home country cooking is always at the heart of any patriotic country home. In the bunkhouses of the West, the cooking was always substantial and plentiful, the serving of it quick and easy, and the table decorations minimal and durable. But cooking, serving, and decorating are becoming more "citified" inside the main houses of today's wild West. The materials are sturdy and recognizable with extra touches that are natural and colorful. Fresh fruit and flowers from the garden are no longer uncommon table decorations.

The West is not the only section of the country that decorates with a patriotic American family style. There are horse farms in the rolling hills of the South, cattle ranches on the islands of Hawaii, and dairy herds along the country back roads of the East. Anywhere there are chickens, dairy cows, cattle, sheep, and pigs, country decorating is a part of everyday living. To soften the harshness of living in the great outdoors, families are combining their heirloom silver and crystal with the ruggedness of tarnished iron and weathered woods.

Down-home country cooking may be natural but it does not need to be traditional in food choice or style. Fresh-squeezed orange juice with a flavoring of white grape juice, gourmet homemade apple/cinnamon bagels, and honey pecan cream cheese make a beginning for any summer morning. The cream cheese is made by mixing softened cream cheese with spun honey and almond flavoring. The napkins are torn from bolts of fabric. The edges are left untouched so that they will fray naturally after a summer of washings.

Family-style decorating with a patriotic interpretation is often eclectic in nature. It means gathering mementos from years of history, collecting displays of artifacts from miles and miles of country landscapes, and blending them together in a house which infers the past is oftentimes more important than the future. The humble collected pieces don't need to match one another, be of the same era, nor be from the same geographical location. They only need to be representative of a land and a history that the occupant holds dear. The pieces used are not always the best of the old; sometimes they are the leftovers that were found in the haylofts of old barns, or in the attics of country homes of people whose grandchildren don't understand their intrinsic values. These treasures, often found at flea markets, have stable values and their beauty is simple, yet profound.

With such eclectic country decorating comes an abandonment of rules and predictability. Old wooden ladders not only can be used as art pieces in their own right but can also display other significant pieces of history. Handwoven Native American blankets, which have become very valuable, can be displayed from the rungs of the ladder.

To make your own wooden ladder, simply cut two wooden staves the desired height of the ladder. Cut the desired number of cross rungs. The rungs can be cut longer for the bottom and taper toward the top. Leather lashing or screws can hold the rungs to the uprights. Full-sized handmade quilts also can be hung on the wall, folded and draped with the blankets on the ladders, or displayed over the back of the naturally covered furniture.

An American flag has been hung and tied back in one corner to give visitors a "glimpse" of another picture of American history.

Country decorating almost always says "sit down and stay awhile." It is the epitome of both comfort and style. And in the picture to the right, as in most cases, comfort equals an abundance of pillows. The two pillows shown here are nontraditional in nature both in their use of American-style fabric and exaggerated ruffles. To make the pillow with the ruffle on the end, cut a piece of printed fleece to the desired width of the pillow and double the desired length of the finished pillow including the ruffle. Fold the fabric in half, wrong sides together, and sew each long edge. Turn inside out, insert pillow form and sew one seam along end.

Outdoor candles used for lighting must be protected from wind and rain. By piercing patterns in the tin sides and top of the candle lantern with an awl or with nails, it is possible to protect the candle and take advantage of the light it produces. If the piercings are designed with a little pattern flair, the candle lantern can add some interesting and authentic flavor to a patriotic decorating theme.

Crocheted chair pads add a down-home flavor. The heart-shaped chair pad at left can repeat a heart design introduced by wallpaper trim or pick up a shape found on the crockery.

At far left, modified star and stripe designs in pillows and napkins support flag themes.

Seaside Country

A Cottage By The Sea

Seaside country decorating always features a variety of books which can be read by family and guests on lazy afternoons or long summer evenings. Include a selection of the classics as well as best-selling paperbacks which can be taken to the beach.

Summers at the beach: fresh air, cool breezes, the sun, the sand, and the sound of the ocean waves. It is a scene that most of us have experienced at one time or another, but not one that we may live with day to day. Just because your country-style home does not have a small garden that soon becomes pure white sand leading to the water's edge, does not mean that you cannot enjoy the comfort and tranquility of seaside-style decorating. Seaside decorating, what is it? How do you define it? How can it be accomplished with ease?

When you think of living by the sea, certain images automatically come to your mind's eye: white cotton sheets, faded-color quilts, piles of pillows, sailboats, collections of seashells, empty hammocks, lots of windows, the afternoon sun, and everything natural. All of which can be had whether your home is by the sea, in the mountains, city, or located in the suburbs.

White slipcovered furniture, with old quilts tossed randomly or piled high on ottomans, is a touch of comfort with just a hint of the ocean. Wooden sailboats which can be painted or have their sails changed with different colors of sailcloth or personalized with the captain's name, are found not only on ocean waves but mountain lakes. Small objects that have a variety of uses are to be found everywhere in any style of country decorating. Rather like the step stool, at right, covered in a vintage white hand towel, that is used in place of a traditional-style end table to hold snacks and cold drinks while you read a book on a lazy afternoon.

Living by the sea makes one think of simple things and lots of them. Collections of everything come to mind. These can be treasures that are found while walking down the beach, mementos purchased while spending lazy afternoons in antique stores, or treasured gifts of thank you given by the many guests who come in reply to your gracious summer weekend invitations.

Collections are much like photographs. Oftentimes you can look at each one and remember where you were, why the time was so very special, and with whom you shared it. For this reason, your favorite keepsakes should be displayed in places where they can be enjoyed daily. It is not necessary to place them where you would expect to see them. Your china cabinet can become the perfect home for your husband's collection of carved figurines, or your dinner-party table can display the array of small crystal bud vases you received—one each Christmas—from your favorite aunt.

Collections can also be used as more utilitarian objects such as the flowerpot pictured to the left. Tiny starfish and shells were attached to a clay pot with quick-dry cement. Such a pot cannot be used out-of-doors unless sealed to prevent the cement from crumbling in the elements. However, it can be used in the kitchen with an insert for not only a tiny blooming violet, but to hold silverware rolled tightly in napkins that are tied with raffia or bright ribbons.

A collection of baskets—either identical or each individual in style—consistent in color, can be stacked one on top of the other in graduated style to serve as an "art" piece, a focal-point, a room divider, as well as providing storage for small items.

Seaside kitchens and cooking areas should be simple, inviting, easy to use, and practically effortless to clean. Blue and white are always a country color combination of choice simply because it brings the outdoors in. It is also easy to change at a moment's notice. It can be made to look like the bright days of summer when sunflowers are added, a little more patriotic when red is the accent color of choice, elegant when crystal and glass add their sparkle, or very French when toile designs are introduced in cushions, window coverings, and wallpaper. Blue and white are a timeless color combination of which you and your guests will never tire.

Let the sea breezes blow through ocean-inspired interiors. Paned windows, simple furnishings, and a conversation area recall port-side cottages.

Decorating shelves can be accomplished by placing items on plainly painted shelves or by designing a backdrop that is subtle yet an intricate aspect of the design. Wallpaper, wrapping paper, and small prints can be adhered with wallpaper paste to the shelf back. If the proper sizing is used, these can be easily removed. Then collected

items such as shells can be stacked or scrapbooks can be displayed in front of the newly designed back panels.

With planning, items displayed on the shelves can be rotated or embellished with theme objects to decorate for various holidays. Showcase a few small framed prints, cream pitchers, wooden toys, or other personal collections.

Home should be a haven for relaxation, renewal, and repose. It does not need to be a showcase of original art or a gallery of the latest high-tech trends. It only needs to be a place where you can decorate with what you love, do what you want, and actually live with a lifestyle that is your definition of comfortable. An integral part of every such comfortable country home should be a bedroom or sitting room that can be used for leisurely private moments. A comfortable chair, favorite personal collections, fresh air, good lighting, windows or doors to open so the sounds of the seasons can be heard, all are essential elements.

Select a focal-point object as your inspiration for color and style. The retro poster of ladies in vintage swimwear sets the beach theme picked up in the striped "beach chair" fabric, the seashell, and the sand-colored raffia beach bag.

Art pieces that are practical can be easily handmade from collections that mean the most to you. A paperweight to secure important papers is made by applying mastic over a glass ball and pressing in an assortment of shells. Greeting cards or small images depicting particularly favorite landmarks in the area, or those which hold special memories, can be cut and framed—or not—for display or to give as gifts for houseguests. Old books, with personal handwritten letters thanking them for accepting your invitation to spend the weekend can be tied with vintage velvet ribbon.

Summers by the sea should be a time when life moves more slowly, when all is warmed by the afternoon rays of the sun, and nights are spent in down-filled beds with mounds of feather pillows and faded vintage quilts. There should be open windows for the sound of the waves and a fan overhead to move the still air on hot summer nights.

Somewhere in everyone's family history there was a time when grandmothers wore modest swimwear and trips to the ocean were a month-long summer affair. These were times when life was less complicated and having fun just seemed easier somehow. Most of us have pictures of just such events and these small photographs, taken by professional photographers, quietly tell the stories of summers spent in another time and place. But for a "picture" to say a thousand words, it need not always be a photograph or a painting. It can be something that was worn and that has been saved for generations in a family trunk tucked away in an attic of the house of a distant relative. Rescue it from obscurity and hang it as you would a cherished photograph.

Creating a country-style look for seaside decorating is easy to do. It is a casual style which is made up of collections, is open to personal interpretation, includes both old and new, and is functional and decorative, all at the same time. The handmade boxes above and to the left are made with images and fabrics that blend with shells that have been collected and saved. The box to the left was painted by an artist as a gift for a friend's wedding. The church is where the friends were married and the shells are from Hawaii where the church is located. The shells were glued to the top of the box so that they could act as the handle and the box was filled with the pictures and mementos from the friend's wedding day. The hatbox above was covered with white embossed wallpaper and painted a basic color. White ribbon was then used to replace the original rope handle, and the box is used to store delicate shells collected on lazy afternoons.

The walls in country homes need not always be covered with wallpaper or paneled with beadboard—something new can be used. First paint the existing wall with the appropriate sealer, then mix a light color in with a plaster medium that is created for textured walls. Texture one section of the wall at a time and as that section is completed, press into place tiny shells in an even row about the height of a chair rail.

Pieces of weathered wood were cut by a professional framer and made into a simple square frame. A small array of shells was glued to the bottom of the frame and then the entire piece was washed with a gray watercolor. A single frame can be constructed to sit on a shelf or a series can be created to cover an entire wall. Make all of the frames identical in size and make enough to cover one premeasured section of wall. In each frame, place pictures that were taken of family and friends during the summer days at the beach.

Summer afternoons at the beach were meant for children to enjoy and make lifetime memories to treasure. An important part of childhood is playing with dollhouses. Here for the little girls who come to stay is a miniature of the room that is theirs for their visit. Complete with hand-painted bed, ruffled comforters, and tiny sailboat, this adorable "little room" can entertain imaginative small guests for hours.

Sea-foam Chic

Formal Country

Formal & Fabulous

Country high style may not be shabby in the least, but despite its formal elegance, it is inviting, comfortable, and relaxed. No doubt the architectural components of the living space will play a tone-setting role in the selection of furniture, its arrangement, and the decorating approach taken in each room's overall detail. The structure of the house itself will usually become a major decorative statement. For example, a brick, stone, or polished-wood wall provides the color and texture upon which a theme is played out against a natural floor.

In a formal room, the seating area may have an inviting rug or carpet, perhaps with a nature-theme pattern such as leaves, flowers, grasses, or animals and birds. In the kitchen or formal dining room, vegetables, grapes, sunflowers, and country scenes are popular imagery for rugs and fabrics used as curtains and to upholster pieces of furniture.

Ceiling treatments are especially interesting in formal country homes, whether they are intimate cottages or luxurious and spacious estates, farms, or ranches. Open beams in formal country homes are generally painted and often embellished, as at far left, with stencil patterns on the cross beams in the style of manor homes and castles in the 1800s. Swedish, English, German, and Arts & Crafts styles perfected ceiling enhancements, and contemporary designers are returning to them for inspiration. Today's beam and ceiling treatments may incorporate words in the form of inspirational quotes, patterns used elsewhere in the room, images depicting family interests, or the formality of a family crest. The crowning touch of a beautiful ceiling, as at far left, expresses refinement through its fabulous detail. Enhanced by a carved mantelpiece, stained-glass windows, and sumptuous textures and comfort in furniture, such fine country rooms welcome us home.

A kitchen or dining room breathes old-world charm into a country home today, with attention to details that evoke a bygone era. Small-paned windows and dark furniture, rich in carved detail, as in the sideboard below, are beautiful and practical. As a storage and display piece for hand-painted pottery it is ideal to establish a theme. The tapestry-style wall covering, painted woodwork, hand-painted ladder-back chairs, floor from a Vermeer painting, and an array of jugs, baskets, food, and wildflowers step us back in "formal home" time.

Country is about the seasonal bounty of nature. Rich color, texture, and rhythm support ample forms with earthy appeal. The Netherlands during Rembrandt's time were rich both literally and figuratively. Their merchant fleets brought back a wealth of coin and worldwide culture. Paintings of the period reflected the formal beauty of starched white linen, elaborate lace, and the ruby tones of ripe fruit, fresh flowers, and abundant exotic foods heaped on pewter plates. To recall that formality and comfort, you can employ warm colors in what we know as an autumn palette. Enhanced by candles, the mood is cozy with rich texture. This hearty palette plays well against white.

Rather than the items themselves, it is in the arrangement of the details that formal country comes to life. Sunflowers, at right, are the epitome of informal blossoms, yet centered and flanked by candles and fruit, they make a formal statement in an antique silver pitcher, as do touches of sculptural relief, abundant fruit and flowers, trailing ribbons, and porcelain, below. Contrasting shiny and soft textures, both visually and tactilely, creates high interest.

As at left, it is the delicacy of fine details that expresses formal elegance. Note how lovely the handle on the porcelain tureen is. Its sculpted attachments to the lid reflect the scalloped wing details of the relief sculpture and the fluted handle on the silver item partially obscured by fruit and flowers. The openwork porcelain fruit bowl has a beautiful rhythm in its rows of designs in fretwork style. The rounded forms of cherub face, tureen lid, and mounds of bulbous fruit shapes are arranged in a harmonious focal point.

Handcarved wild-cherry wood paneling, relief sculpture on bar posts, above, and layers of cornice work are opulent in a formal country home. Add granite or marble wet-bar counters and tabletops for country on the formal "grand" scale. With this style, cut glass at the windows, lead crystal and silver barware, elaborately carved sofa tables, and the subtle lighting to support the ruby-toned hardwoods promise all the comforts of an English manor. Tapestry pillows, above right, gold-leafed picture frames, and formally arranged furniture on fine carpets set a relaxed but undisputably formal country drawing-room ambience. Note how the ceiling, at right, embraces the room with the same robust wild-cherry wood treatment to catch the glow.

The formal country boudoir is more than a bedroom. The resting retreat for a man or a woman will be a mixture of restorative spa and masterfully orchestrated charm. Textures and colors merge in a sensual environment of splendor and comfort. A gilded, bas-relief-framed mirror at the bedside or on the bureau holds miniature decanters of lotions and perfumes to indulge in before bedtime. An elegantly dressed bed is piled high with pillows of velvet, lace, linen—perhaps with mother-of-pearl button closures, brocades, and satin. Tassels and beads may appear. Tables can be draped with folds of similar softening fabrics. Colors are restful. If carved marble mantelpieces are not among the architectural elements of the formal bedroom, the look can be created with a bit of ingenuity and effort, as at right. Cherub plaques in embossed relief may be purchased, or they may be cast in plaster or handmade paper. For these at right, two 3½" plaster cherubs were affixed to two 8½" x 8½" x ¼" plywood tiles with craft glue. To add "C" shape scroll embellishments, fill a cake-decorating bag half full with joint compound and using various tips, create pleasing arrangements of scrolls, buds, flowers, and leaves for a rococo effect. Allow to dry and harden, or bake on low in an oven before painting, glazing, and sealing with acrylic products, according to manufacturer's directions.

The plaster and joint-compound cherub tiles make stunning wall plaques, but they are also charming as architectural accents to mantels, shelf supports, or for above-door or window cornices.

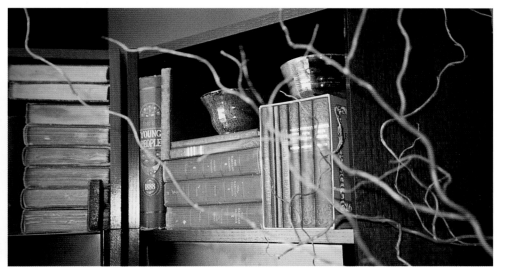

Great design is in the details, and the more unique, the more exciting and memorable they will be. Formal country gives rise to the unusual in storage and display solutions that are one of a kind, usually the result of some favored personal items. Miniature easels, leather-bound books in artful arrangements, antique handles, knobs, bookends—and out-of-the-ordinary items used as bookends—are ideas you can use with what you already own. For the dazzling jewelry storage solution, at left, use a group of painted frames backed with fabric-covered foam-core board and bead knobs.

Eclectic Country

Collector Style

"Eclectic" by definition is what appears to be the best of various styles and is composed of elements drawn from several sources, . . . making eclectic country decorating the best of everything and anything. Most collectors are eclectic in nature. They collect everything from African fabrics to French porcelain, English laces to Italian glassware. They arrange each piece carefully in their homes in a way that always "works," even when you can't believe that it will. The reason that it does is because personal collections all have a unifying theme, though sometimes the collector cannot identify exactly what that theme may be. The reason may be nothing more than every item is loved by the collector who bought it; and because we each have an individual style, it is that particular style which is present in everything that attracts us.

This eclectic country room stars pure white cotton bedding, primitive African fabrics, and rustic Western furniture. In traditional decorating styles, this combination wouldn't work. However, when styled by a collector who is fascinated by all three, it offers an unexpected simplicity and comfort that is elegant, yet unrefined.

71

The contradiction of materials is what gives this room its drama. Pure cotton fabrics, which are bleached white and softened from continued washings, are styled together with roughly woven, brightly dyed fabrics that are Indian in origin. The woven pillows were made from a large bed throw that was worn in several places and could no longer be used. If these colors should bleed onto the stark white cottons, the color can be removed by using a chlorinated laundry bleach or borax product. Sunlight will further lighten whites to keep them crisp.

The attention to detail is an essential part of creating a country home—be it cozy, quaint, primitive, or eclectic. There are no strict constraints about what works and what doesn't, nor any rules or regulations to follow about what finishes, furniture, or fabrics constitute country style and how they should be properly combined.

Country doors with primitive handles and a coatrack that is both decorative and functional are part of this overall country design. Even the state-of-the-art heating system has been disguised with rustic wooden louvered grates.

The arching flower spray above the door, at left, is made from the flowers native to the local area. These natural materials can be easily designed for any room in any size. First make a twig arch for a framework. Use a stick the width of the doorway, tie or tack twigs with numerous branches onto each end of the horizontal stick. Bend twigs into an appropriately sized arching spray and wire them together with craft wire. Weave in additional twigs to form a sturdy framework on which to glue your choice of dried flowers, foliage, herbs, and ribbons. Hot-glue an assortment of dried flowers and foliage onto the twigs. The entire spray does not need to be covered with flowers because the twigs themselves can be an interesting design element. Hang the finished spray above the doorway, using rustic nails, fanciful vintage knobs, or unique decorative hooks.

To clean a dried flower arrangement, place it outside in a stiff wind to allow dust and cobwebs to be blown away or use camera air spray.

Due to the absence of rules and formal guidelines, creating a country sensibility is one of the most difficult aspects of eclectic country decorating. To help understand the essence of what you are trying to create, be aware of the different periods of history, the influences of different cultures, and the essences of different styles which please you. Choose colors that have earthy overtones created with natural vegetable dyes, choose materials that are untouched except by time and weather, and select furniture pieces that fulfill your needs and are the best of a variety of styles. Do not make your lighting centralized and harsh, but dispersed and more natural. Repeat several aspects of your decorating—there is power in numbers; and above all else, make certain that each piece of furniture is comfortable and wonderfully worn.

Country Sensibility

Simplicity can speak for itself, evoking a mood that is often impossible to achieve under other conditions. The simple use of woven African fabrics hung or draped over the tops of doors creates a subtle design of color and texture.

The beaded rosary was made with hand-shaped wooden beads and a primitively carved wooden cross strung on a black cord. Setting a "primary culture" theme is quite achievable with artifacts and fabrics from around the world. Combine them with rustic wood, hand-wrought metal, and woven fibers.

Without rules for what is permissible to put together in a room, it's a delightful creative experience to launch your own style. Coordinate fabrics, wood, pottery, and so forth by selecting items that share the same color palette, patterns, and handmade appearance. Play with contrasts in textures and forms that create the drama so apparent in art, music, dance, literature, and culture of ethnic groups you particularly admire.

Upper Left: This dark wall of rough cedar is softened and made surprising by the hanging piece of handwoven fabric next to the gilded-gold frame. Neither would ordinarily be hung separately on this wall in this manner, but together they make an elegant statement of contradiction. The tissue holder is a piece of antler.

Upper Right: This simple wooden shelf has been adorned with twigs collected in the countryside, broken into different lengths and adhered to the bottom of the shelf with a thick coating of wood glue. They also could have been secured individually by drilling holes before gluing. The outer edge of the shelf was then wrapped with a narrow strip of glued-into-place birch bark. Mount shelf with screws or bonding liquid.

Lower Left: A variety of container sizes and shapes is used for the essentials in the powder room. The washcloths are folded into a rustic urn, and the small bowl can hold jewelry and small valuables.

More-sophisticated Victorian serving pieces are added to this rustic shelf, which offers a kind of diversity that is striking and distinct. The silver is not polished because the tarnished finish is more in keeping with the grayed cedar walls. The shelf is an old piece of wood which was planed and sanded on one side, then attached to the wall above primitive wooden dowels that are used to hang robes and towels. Candles are placed throughout the bathroom to offer a warm softer light and a welcoming fragrance to this rustic powder room.

Because this bath area is so secluded it is also used as a sanctuary—a place to revitalize the body and the soul. It is a place where the combination of tile, wood, masonry, and sterling accessories presents an eclectic blend of comfort, security, and solitude. The result is a space which brings peace to anyone trying to escape a frenzied and often confused world.

It is easy to make a natural twig wreath, as at left. To begin, gather a bundle of twigs, each approximately 24"–36" in length. Soak overnight in water to soften. Take 5–10 twigs in hand and wrap with craft wire. Add a new bundle of twigs about ⅓ the way up the first bundle, and wire them to only some of the original twigs. Sculpt and form the twigs as you bend and wrap them into the wreath shape. Wire the top and bottom portions of the twigs together, allowing some of the twigs to splay out. This adds a more contemporary design element to the wreath. Allow to dry before hanging on the wall. Leave the wreath plain, decorate it with native flowers, or nestle a much-loved collectible inside. Secure it tightly to the twigs with floral wire so it will not be knocked off and broken.

Fine porcelain displayed on a distressed-wood shelf is appealing in this contradictory composition. To distress the wood on an aged armoire or hutch for this style accent, simply use coarse sandpaper or an electric sander and sand with the grain of the wood until portions of the wood show through the paint. Edges, corners, and handles are areas to target for distressing, as these locations are where paint naturally wears off first. When the piece shows adequate "aging," protect the newly exposed wood with several coats of furniture polish.

Romance is an essential element of eclectic decorating that is gained from the embellishment of exquisite details that are both decorative and stylized. It is the touch of lace—sometimes used as a table cover, sometimes as a bedroom throw—the ruggedly aged finish of an old water pump no longer in working condition, or the delicately refined patina of the tarnished silver serving set that speaks of stately candlelit dinners and grand ballrooms. We particularly appreciate the simple elegance of these romantic vintage belongings when we combine them, by contrast, in a contemporary time and place.

Vintage fabrics, crazy quilts, and flea-market finds can set an enviable theme in a contemporary interior. Using them creatively as table drapery, pillows, and textured throws gives colorful flavor to a neutral-toned setting. Throws may be handwoven or patched-together pieces of old satins and velvets, with delicate and decorative stitches for embellishments. Handmade items are indicative of their time, place, and maker. Such pieces are sometimes discarded as too worn or too unrefined to be of any value. However, sometimes they are given from mother to daughter or native to visitor as an expression paying tribute to that which is made lovingly by both the heart and the hand for someone held in high esteem. Such artistic items become focal point magic.

Lower right: Native American pottery pieces are set on small basket lids to visually soften the space between wood and pottery and to offer protection for the wooden shelf or furniture.

Three different times, two different cultures, and one collector who has found success in combining them to create a unique personal country style. This hand-carved western bowl, filled with often-used and much-worn baseballs, is an unlikely companion to the stone grinding wheel. Such a display is evidence that collectors of today have a bounty from which to choose and an abandon with which to combine their collections. Each is a cherished object—enjoyed for reasons that may be unknown to strangers—and in this home, displayed in a manner that needs no explanation.

Books are used often and everywhere in every style of country decorating. In an eclectic country library, the books are often too worn to actually be read again; these are used instead as decorative elements. Above, these rare and once often-read books act as a backdrop to a vintage porcelain figurine and a rustic-framed print of a dancer. Books such as these should be cared for by avoiding sources of heat, humidity, and dirt. Sunlight causes fading, as does florescent lighting and smoke—which should be avoided as it causes rapid paper damage.

The rustic elements in an eclectic style are as varied among themselves as are the variety of collections they surround. They are selected for decorative use as the result of the emotional need for balance. These accessories of nature are used to enhance a room: stone, feathers, wood, leather, and rusted metal. Used in pleasing combination, they are Mother Nature's balancing accents in the midst of our high-tech civilization.

Have you observed that there are some rooms that you enter for the first time and you feel both a spiritual and visual pleasure? Their warmth and eclectic charm are the rustic elements that create a comfortable and cozy home. These rooms create personal space while offering a warm welcome to friends and family. They celebrate a connection to nature which offers us peace and tranquility.

After a lifetime of trends, fads, and designer-driven styles, it is at last with eclectic country decorating that rooms are considered home and not taken too seriously. Pieces of the past are incorporated to remind us that the "basics" are still very important to our sensibilities.

NO SPITTING AT TABLES WALLS & FLOORS

By The Gracious Ordinance Of The Honourable Lords Of The Royal Courts Of Justice
LONDON ENGLAND dated 1871

Evenings spent outdoors—is there any better way to describe the comfort of country? Whether you are sitting by yourself doing nothing more than listening to the sound of nature, watching the sun set on a quiet porch with a friend, or preparing to set the picnic table for dinner with silver candlesticks and rustic wooden plates, the essence of all that is nature is what makes you decorate in natural country style. The wooden table can be covered with woven African blankets and the wooden pots on the porch can be filled with ferns because ferns are rarely seen in such rugged surroundings. The light on the table is turned on after dark to emit a kind of soft romantic glow. The chairs introduce a new style—one that is of bleached wood such as an Adirondack chair. Nothing is expected, but all is natural, and when placed with a loving hand, suggests a quiet contentment that is only found in secret places that offer the comfort of a country home—a place we'd all like to be.

Rustic Country

Country All The Way

Rustic decorating in ranch-inspired homes is not unlike the rules for seaside decorating. It is the decorative elements that create the retreat, not the address. Components are all as natural as possible: rough rock, smooth river-run stone, warm leather upholstery, rough-hewn wood architectural and furniture elements, baskets fashioned from twigs, hand-woven wall hangings and throws, animal skins, antlers, natural-fiber fabrics, clay pots, and metal.

What would rustic living be without charm and comfort? Barren and boring! Enliven country rustic with chic style. Incorporate fine craftsmanship in practical and beautiful enrichments: a polished brass bar sink; glistening counters and tiles; heirloom porcelain, lamps, or quilts; and the surprise of an indoor weather vane or an antler wine rack.

Whether entertaining guests or enjoying a private candlelight dinner for two, rustic doesn't eliminate elegance. Set an inviting tone with a hardwood or painted table, simple crystal stemware, layered table settings with wheel-thrown pottery plates, pewter or silver flatware, a bowl of wildflowers as a center-piece, and perhaps Western bandannas for napkins. Cushion antique wooden chairs with decorative pillows or loom-woven mats. Keep the food hearty; present it with all the attention to detail you would use in a fancy restaurant, while your country atmosphere is relaxed and nourishing for body and soul.

A country bedroom in rustic style is more about comfort and beauty than any room in the house. Rest and restoration after an outdoor day begin with a spacious room that could feature hardwood or wide-pine floors and sturdy painted-wood furniture. It may, as the room at right, include a bed with a massive hand-painted headboard piled with an abundance of luxurious pillows and quilts. Nature-themed art appears with robust or delicate style and colors of earth and sky.

Add decorating touches of leather goods, such as saddles, bridles, boots, riding crops, boxes, and books that are ideal for pulling such a look together.

Let in light and air, but control how much with curtains, louvered shutters, or slatted-wood blinds for comfortable sleeping year-round. A paddle fan in the ceiling will disperse summer air, while in the winter a bedroom fireplace's heat can be sent around the house by the same fan. Bedrooms opening onto balconies and porches are especially desirable for natural rest in an outdoor atmosphere.

The country bath has taken on day-spa ambience. Surrounded in comfort and beauty, it's more than a place to "wash up." Stone, terra-cotta, or ceramic tile surfaces are easy to clean and texturally in harmony with the natural environment. Themed accents may include framed pastoral or Western scenes or family portraits, hand-painted sinks, candles, wooden and ceramic sculptures, Western-bar-style swinging shower or entry doors, stylish lamps not usually found in a bath, jugs of wildflowers, baskets, and mirrors to double the space. Plumbing fixtures come in a variety of retro styles and materials, such as bronze and gun-metal finishes, copper, porcelain, and pewter. Finding the perfect faucets to harmonize with other rustic elements in the room is primarily a matter of deciding how much you want to spend. Basins with hand-painted images can be purchased or, for the talented, created. For guests, fill a basket, as at right, with overnight necessities such as washcloths, hand towels, soaps, body lotions, toothpaste, and shampoo.

Embody the strength of rusted iron and rough-hewn logs with the wisdom of aged wooden furniture and outdoor life-styles. No matter how cozy or spacious your rustic retreat may be, there is a sensible approach to be found in decorating it to meet your physical and spiritual needs. Let the outdoors flow in and out like breathing. Arrange favorite objects in a comfortable nature setting to make every guest feel right at home.

Nothing says country chic like weathered-wood exteriors and outdoor furniture with the patina of time. Unfinished deck and log railings, at left, are as welcoming in their unpretentious state as the charming log cabin's covered porch with brimming flower boxes and its chunky club chairs inside.

Bunkhouse meets cowboy-movie nostalgia in the country bedroom above. Sturdy Mission-style lines in the bed are strongly masculine, supported by bold plaids, plenty of wood and "horsey" accents, along with strong colors in hues of blue. Creative use of barbed wire for a picture hanger, a cowhide-covered journal, and a horse collar once used for pulling heavy loads now pull the country-ranch theme together. A feminine touch balances the room with the Western film star photo transfers used on the throw pillows, the double-skirted side table, and the soft wall color.

Miniature furniture collectibles create delightful vignettes when displayed on windowsills, fireplace mantels, side tables, and shelves. Guests will enjoy the fun of noticing the tiny details and scale compared to the rest of the room. Miniatures make for a nearly irresistible dollhouse interaction between guest and "little room" conversational grouping. If you don't want the tiny items handled, it may be necessary to display them high enough so that it is obvious they are for visual pleasure only; or you may choose to put them into a display case so that there is no confusion.

Weathered wood and vintage items are comfortable together in texture, color, theme, and practicality. An old wooden box with vintage stair railings serves as a window box filled with colorful annuals, above left, while an aging wooden spool which once held wire makes a unique plant holder for trailing foliage. The peeling twig chair, above right, appears to have grown of its own accord in this garden spot. At left, hang hats and fishing gear on unique pegs. A flat iron can be pressed into service as a bookend.

Recycled objects bring new life to the garden when given a second chance to play a starring role as focal points. The enamel kitchen pot, at right, no longer serves up savories from the stove, but is a fitting flowerpot when perched on a weathered stump. Its handles make moving it to face the sun easy, and its rusty patina is a textural delight when crowned with geraniums and ivy. Below left, the Purple Martin apartment house in a sunflower garden is both beautiful and practical. Voracious Martins and their young consume great quantities of mosquitoes and other insect pests. An old wooden door, below right, becomes a country-chic focal point when embellished with a cluster of colorful dried Indian corn strung with cord on a nail.

Nothing says "relax" like a rocking chair which makes a friendly creaking sound when it moves. Place it strategically on a porch or in the garden with a view of a pond, trickling fountain, brook, once-popular fishing hole, or a field of wildflowers. Let the silence be broken only by prairie winds, droning bees, grazing cattle, the whinny of a horse, or the sporadic far-off wail of a freight train. In such a setting, hands that worked hard during the daylight hours and weary spirits can rest with the setting of the evening sun.

Collector's Country

A Country Bazaar

Vintage collectibles and fabrics blend nostalgia and utility with authentic retro charm. Kitchens like the ones at left and right make the most of pegs and shelving for storing pots, pans, hand towels, and dinnerware. When selecting collectible items from country bazaars and flea markets, look for those you can actually use as well as display. Oilcloth, flower-print seed and feed bags, bordered hand towels, and old table linens can be used "as is" or refashioned into shelf liners, chair pads, and curtains.

Colorful storage containers, as the red and green glass ones at left, can tie a room together visually when not in use in the refrigerator. Rag rugs, trestle tables, cast-iron cookware, enamel and tinware, pottery cookie jars, and Bakelite®-handled cooking utensils add to the look of country "kitsch." Whether you collect salt and pepper shakers from the '20s to '50s, or vintage tea towels, display them in ways that they become the theme of your room as well as being usable.

When collectors of tables as classic as this one make such a find, the enameled metal top comes home to serve myriad uses. Pull out the drawer for flatware or napkin rings, roll out a pie crust, or enjoy breakfast or lunch on its easy-clean surface. Children find its surface perfect for play dough and craft projects. Practical furniture designers of the past knew what they were about.

Open shelving, right up to the rafters or ceiling cornices, is a collector's edge when it comes to display. Antique glass, tinware, and pastry and cooking tools can be grouped to create the visual interest ordinarily reserved for curtains and art.

Simple shutters, at left, offer all of the light control one could want, while simplifying the room down to square ceiling tiles, plaid wallpaper behind plain-wood shelves, and minimal colors.

The colors in the room come from the collected items themselves. All other surfaces are wood, metal, or painted white. This design approach makes certain that collectibles do not become a chaotic jumble, but instead, form a deliberate display with similar items in groups. Note how the shelf of canning jars is arranged beneath a shelf of clear glass bottles in various sizes. Visually and physically heavier items, such as mortar and pestle, flat irons, and so forth are on the bottom shelf.

On the counter, a row of framed collectible images is treated the same and leaned, rather than hung on the wall to harmonize with the prominent print grouping above the kitchen table shown at far left. However, the wall of the shelving could as easily have been pegboard above the counter and home to a collection of antique cookie cutters or butter molds hung on a child's wooden clothespins strung with ribbon or antique cotton clothesline. Other items can be stored in accessible bins and baskets below the counter. Wainscoting supports a new 'old' look.

Nothing excites a collector of antique kitchen or garden tools more than the delightful shapes, textures, and functions of metal memorabilia. Note the rake head, at left, hung on the wall 'teeth' side out, to make a unique row of pegs for an array of tools. Scoops, egg beaters, cookie sheets, egg separators, spatulas, and items we rarely need anymore suddenly take on new importance. The squares of the wallpaper, or a striped pattern, make a simple backdrop for such varied shapes and textures as these. They would be lost or compete with a heavily designed paper, such as scenics, flowers, animals, fruits, or vegetables. An old wooden rolling pin becomes a towel hanger, at left, or joins beribboned sister items in a bucket (below). Edged quilt blocks, at right, are decorative drama as shelf liners or draped on a pulled-out drawer.

Note how the design of this wall of collectibles has been created with a pleasing arrangement which includes canning-jar lids to fill in the visual "holes" made when hanging odd-shaped items. The triangle formed by the rolling-pin hanger is repeated nicely with the simple technique of displaying the cookie sheet as a diamond, instead of a square. Its lower right edge is parallel to the hanger as it crosses the wallpaper squares.

This harmonious grouping of ironstone cups and saucers with their magenta-pink pattern mixes beautifully with hemmed quilt squares in related hues. The arrangement of the quilt-block points leads our eyes down to the candle and blue dinnerware, finishing with more quilt pieces as mats below.

On these pages, Shaker-simple wood furnishings and plain white walls are an appropriate background for a glowing collection of pewter dinnerware and serving pieces, tart pans, crockery, skeleton keys, candlesticks, and assorted basketry.

The pie safe with its punch-pattern in the popular turn-of-the-twentieth-century pineapple design, at far left, is the focal point of this wall arrangement, made harmonious in theme and concept by the surrounding antique pie tins. A few are hung on the pie safe's outer walls, and the remainder are secured to the wall of the room by various wire handles and hangers. Each pie pan is a comfortable distance from the others to reinforce the stability of the design and the era they reflect.

Part of the joy collectors have in scouring shops and bazaars for the memorabilia of bygone days is the simplicity the objects portray. The sideboard with its hutch-style top, near left, would seem overwhelmed with this much dinnerware if it were not a unified collection of polished pewter. It could as easily have been a selection of copper, wood, or enamelware, or a pleasing arrangement of milk glass, rubyware, all-white porcelain, pickle containers, compotes, or pedestal banana boats in cut crystal.

Note how even the pewter-toned mat on the framed sampler to the right of the hutch is keyed to the collection, as opposed to any other decorative element in the room. Such subtleties are the essence of thoughtful design which contains the collection, whatever it may be, to the focal point, rather than create a hodgepodge of many items poorly displayed.

For the quilt collector, wall hangings such as this 16-patch design combine beautifully with a pinwheel-design quilt used as a throw for an antique chair. The quilt-patch pattern in the floor covering grounds the theme and is augmented by the fabric colors picked up in the mosaic vase, with its colorful assortment of beach finds and trinkets. Keeping all the other elements simple works best. Using a formal marble pedestal to hold the vase is a pleasing surprise.

The most difficult-to-display collections are the ones that have a profusion of bright color, shape and size variety, and theme change going on within them so that grouping them may be a challenge. If the items are relatively small in scale, as the Smokey the Bear toys at left, for example, then one set of shelves may be your answer.

Here the back and sides of the shelving are used for books, posters, badges, and pins, while the shelves each serve to house mini focal points which tell a story. The theme of Smokey, his Jeep, and his friends unifies the collection. A glass case front protects so many tiny pieces from loss and dust build-up. Doll, car, truck, military, and movie action figures may be displayed just as successfully.

The personal ways that people combine their inherited or found treasures is what makes a home so interesting and unique. Above, a quilt is a unifying background for a collection of hand-made throw pillows, and a tray of small items.

The white airedale pup stands out as a focal point on a white shelf because it is wisely backed with a black vintage tray for contrast. Favorite books, a mini license plate, and a tiny shoe help the toy dog express a "childhood memories" theme.

Whether Amish in design, of Norwegian rosemaling, Santa Fe in style, or Pennsylvania Dutch in theme, a keepsake trunk from any background or culture is worthy of becoming a centerpiece in any room. The hand-painting, carving, or parquet work deserves good lighting to be appreciated. If collecting sea or carriage trunks, hope chests, and the like is a hobby of yours, consider using one to be the inspiration for all the rooms in your home. Use a trunk's strong form as a visual anchor and support with one or more "chunky" items to balance it. To enhance your wooden or wicker chest, connect its colors in the room.

A collection of family photos is sometimes difficult to arrange effectively. With a variety of frame shapes and sizes, it is wise to create a template using craft-paper which allows you to arrange until you're pleased. You can add a mirror or two to fill in a grouping if necessary for balance. Note how the lowest row of frames line up to allow the space required for the wall's furniture and display items below.

White Is Crisp For Country

White is a classic country color for all seasons, a color that is timeless, and a color whose many different shades and tints allow you to feel completely comfortable. You can rest your tired soul in a cool bedroom painted the softest shade of summer white with a tiny hint of robin's-egg blue, or you can wrap yourself in thick white towels that are the hue of freshly fallen snow. White is minimal yet luxurious, it is classic yet contemporary, it is calming yet daring. White is pure, simple, elegant, and fresh. White is a color that is easy to come back to, . . . regardless of the influential colors of today's trends. When your mood changes, introduce a different color in a few gentle accents.

The textures of white can range from the smooth and sleek of white porcelain pitchers to the rough feel of weathered wood or the softness of pure white cotton hand towels. When decorating with white there are literally hundreds of shades from warm to cool to choose from. Blending and mixing them together gives a white room its personality, as shown in this designer's collection of vintage kitchenware displayed on primitive wooden shelves. Warm tints of white combine to make one feel cozy and comfortable. While the whites give a clean and tidy feeling, the room is casually disorganized enough to be welcoming rather than overly fussy and pristine.

Interest is added to the stair-landing with a wooden birdhouse, oversized boxes filled with artfully pruned topiaries, and a diverse array of containers overflowing with ivy that add outdoor interest to the garden accent of a handpainted ewe. Landings may be considered a kind of secret hideaway where scenes for each of the seasons can be designed and displayed with a creative attention to detail.

This white-on-white interior is easily transformed by the changing of the seasons. Cool fresh whites are accented here by only the pale green colors of spring; however, with the addition of a red ribbon on the lamb, holly berries, fur boughs, and a jolly Santa figure, the holidays would be festively announced.

131

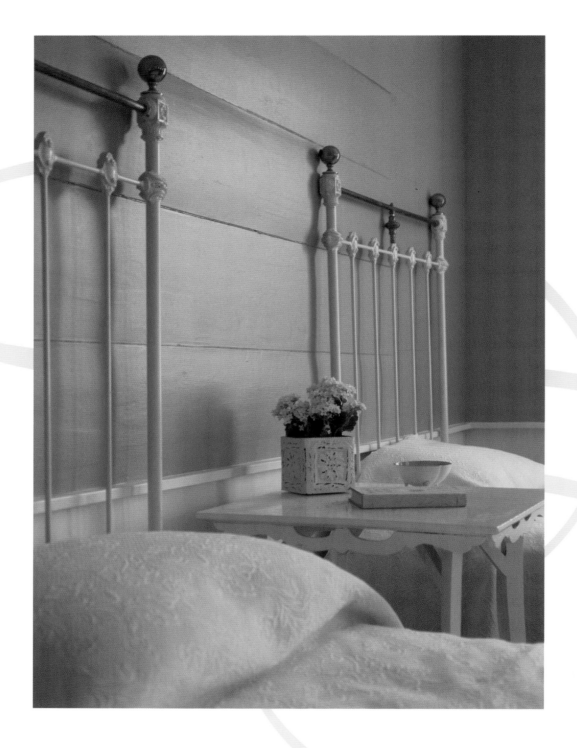

The spare beauty of these white-enameled iron headboards against a simple wall have an architectural appeal. Their strong verticals play nicely against the wainscotting and horizontal boards of the unusual wall. Simple white bed linens allow the lacy effect of the side table's gingerbread trim to take center stage. This room appears to welcome with serenity and restfulness, proving a minimalist design approach has true elegance.

Decorating with white is interesting because it puts the accent on texture and design. To the left, this birdhouse was constructed from old pieces of weathered wood, discarded scraps of architectural molding, and broken finials which were painted white and distressed. A metal picture frame was sprayed with white enamel and glued around the entrance. A perch was created by affixing a recycled drawer pull to an antique fluted-metal pipe fitting, then painted. There is charm in all the different details displayed in relief, one against another.

Below, the head- and footboards for this guest-room bed were constructed from wooden slats purchased at a lumberyard and originally intended for fence making. The designer wished for everything to be as fresh and new as a spring day; so the paint was not distressed but applied with several coats of enamel. Crisp, white cotton bed linens make this a wonderful welcome for any overnight guest. The "fence" shadow patterns enhance a spring theme.

Country and vintage styles merge beautifully in the display items at left and above. Shells, hearts, roses, lace, porcelain, and an abundance of delicate detail are "ribboned" exquisitely together. In concert, they return us to an era when, even in the country, work halted for tea time. Plates of home-made treats were brought into the parlor and set on a table where a jug of freshly picked roses were reflected in etched, elegantly framed mirrors. Though the porcelain plates have relief patterns of flowers which add interest to lacy pierced work, they could be handpainted to fit a theme within a room. Why not display them in their simplicity arranged with ribbons on pegs in a dining area?

In the bath at right, echo repeating plate displays with an arrangement of mismatched mirror shapes, all painted warm white.

To create a wall or mantel arrangement of framed "art", select matching store-bought frames and a collection of buttons, cards, old lace, pressed nature materials, baby spoons, costume jewelry, or ribbons. To plan, arrange your treasures symmetrically or asymmetrically within the frame until they please you. Cut foam board to fit the frame for backing. Cut mat board to fit the frame and cut openings—little windows—for your arrangement. Cut white linen or other textured-weave fabric to fit the entire mat, and using reposition-able spray mount, attach fabric to the mat. Cut the window openings in the fabric with a craft knife, making X cuts from corner to corner. To prevent fraying, do not cut too close to the window corners. Fold the fabric into the openings and through to the back of the mat, stretching to cover edges evenly. Secure with glue. Cut a smaller piece of fabric to fit behind the cut-out window in the mat and spray mount it to the foam-board backing. Secure the mats into their frames and position items to be displayed in the window openings. Sew or glue the items onto the foam backing within their framed mats. A three, six, or traditional 9-patch quilt-block arrangement for the framed group on your wall would make a stunning focal point in an all-white room.

To create the windowpane collection of DaVinci portraits, below, scan and photocopy selected images onto decal paper, using a color copier, even if the image is black and white. Soak decal paper in warm water for one minute. Transfer to front of glass, following manufacturer's instructions. Squeegee out air bubbles, let dry for 24 hours, then apply clear matte water-based varnish. For frame, paint with base color that allows top-color cracks to show through. Let dry. Apply crackle medium for a vintage look. Use brush or sponge to apply a thin coat for fine cracks or a thick coat for large ones. Dry 1–4 hours.

The twill-sashed panel curtains, above, are strips of translucent fabric hemmed and hung from two lengths of copper-tubing rods mounted on grooved wooden blocks. They create an arresting focal point and are practical at the same time. As the sun moves around trees or building, the panels can be lengthened or shortened to eliminate glare on TV or computer screens or to offer privacy, while allowing a maximum amount of light. Measure the width and length of the window. Divide the width by the number of desired panels. Add 4" to that quotient for each panel width. Add 6" to the window length. Multiply the "total length" by the desired number of panels for panel fabric. Double the total length and multiply by the desired number of panels for twill tie strips. Cut each panel and each tie. Sew a 4" pocket at the top of each panel to accommodate tubing. Center and drape one twill tie from front to back over each 4" pocket and sew in place along pocket seamline. Sew a 1" pocket at the hem to accommodate dowel. Cut one ½" diameter dowel to the width of each panel. Hang the panels, staggering back to front on their respective rods. Insert dowel into each panel hem for weight. To allow natural sunlight in, roll up and tie.

The white metal faux flowers, above, make delightful garden accents when "planted" among nature's flowers at a turning point on a path, as clues to an upcoming focal point, or near a lantern where they will appear to glow in the moonlight. At left, to add a festive air for a garden baby shower, display an heirloom quilt decorated with a beautiful white infant outfit pinned on a dainty ribbon clothesline.

Acknowledgments

I'd like to thank everyone at Chapelle, especially Jo Packham, whose creativity and energy I respect and admire, and without whom this book would not have been possible.

I'd also like to thank my family and friends, especially my parents and brothers for their love and support throughout the years.

Denise McGann

Credits

Corbis Images (©2000) 16

Diane Lace 57u, 57l

Getty Images, Inc. (©1999–2002) 132, 133l

Jesse Walker 1, 6, 7, 10, 12, 15, 17, 19, 20, 22–23, 25–26, 28ul, 30, 31u, 32ll, 32ur, 33–34, 36, 38l, 39, 41–42, 43ul, 43l, 44–46, 47l, 48, 49u, 50, 53–54, 58– 60, 61u, 61l, 79u, 79c, 79l, 94, 110, 112, 120, 126, 129–131, 135, 142ur

Jo Packham 51ur, 67l, 67ur, 67c, 67lr, 73l, 74u, 75l, 75ur, 75lr, 81l, 83ul, 83ll, 83lr, 85ur, 86, 107l, 106u, 106ll, 106lr, 133u

Kevin Dilley 9, 14u, 14l, 18r, 21l, 21ur, 21lr, 24u, 28ur, 29l, 29c, 29r, 31l, 40u, 40l, 47lr, 49ll, 49lr, 51ul, 51ll, 52u, 52l, 64, 65ur, 65lr, 66, 68, 70–71, 72l, 72ur, 72lr, 73u, 74l, 76ul, 76ll, 76ur, 77, 78l, 78ur, 80, 81u, 82, 84, 85lr, 87, 88u, 88ll, 89u, 89l, 90, 92, 95–100, 101u, 101l, Kevin

Dilley (continued) 102u, 102l, 103–104, 105ur, 105ul, 105l, 114–115, 116l, 118–119, 121–125 134l, 134r, 136, 137u, 137ll, 139, 142ll

Leslie M. Newman 35ur, 107r, 108u, 108ll, 108lr, 109, 116r

PhotoDisc, Inc. Images (©1999) 43ur, 88lr

Ryne Hazen 35ll, 117, 128, 138, 144

Scot Zimmerman 2–5, 47, 56, 62, 63ul, 63ur, 63l, 93, 113

The publishers wish to thank the following people for allowing us extensive access in photographing their homes:

Kathryn Elliot
Linda & David Durbano
Phyllis Rogler
Mel Kemp

About The Author

Photo by Bob Brody

Born and raised on Long Island and currently living in New York City, Denise McGann has reviewed hundreds of books every year on home decorating, as Editor-in-Chief of Country Homes & Gardens Book Club®. She had not come across a book focusing on country style and what it means today. This book gives suggestions and ideas for new ways to interpret country style and encourages you to experiment with this type of decorating.

Appreciation

For use of their products, the publishers wish to thank:

Arte Halica, 225 Fifth Ave. Ste. 1225, NY, NY 10010
Chalices p. 64

Barloga Studios, 1933 Davis St. #287, San Leandro, CA 94577
Replica French sign p. 21all

Barreveld, 3027 Route 9, Cold Spring, NY 10516
Dove soap dish p. 21ul

Foreside, 33 Hutcherson Dr., Gorhan, ME 040381
Metal flowers p. 139

Garden Party, 422 Websterville Rd, Barre, VT 05641
Bottle with glass grapes p. 21l

Lafco, 200 Hudson St., NY, NY 10013-1807
Scent bottles p. 64

La Lavande, 5221 Central Ave. #7, Richmond, CA 94804
Wire soap holder p. 21lr

Ruby & Begonia, P.O. Box 9252, Ogden, UT 84409
*Framed expressions p. 28 ur, Miniature bed p. 52ll,
Pillow p. 64, Miniature beds p. 105 all, Framed items p. 136*

Tag, 1730 West Whrightwood, Chicago, IL 60614-1914
Ceramic candle urn p. 21lr

Theodoras Collection, P.O. Box 825, Matthews, NC 28106
DaVinci prints in windowpane p. 137ll

Two's Company, P.O. Box 5302, NY, NY 10087-5302
Ceramic pitchers p. 47lr, Ceramic plates p. 134r

Index